Some Assembly Required

Some Assembly Required

POEMS BY

George Bradley

ALFRED A. KNOPF

NEW YORK

2001

THIS IS A BORZOI BOOK
PUBLISHED BY ALFRED A. KNOPF

Copyright © 2001 by George Bradley
All rights reserved under International and Pan-American Copyright
Conventions. Published in the United States by Alfred A. Knopf, a
division of Random House, Inc., New York, and simultaneously in
Canada by Random House of Canada Limited, Toronto. Distributed
by Random House, Inc., New York.

www.aaknopf.com

Knopf, Borzoi Books, and the colophon are registered trademarks of
Random House, Inc.

The following publications first printed the poems here indicated: *Hartford Courant:* "Mud Season"; *New England Review:* "Christmas Storm Down East"; *The New Yorker:* "Millrace," "In an Old Garden," "A Scrap of Sky"; *The Paris Review:* "Nabu-Kudurri-Usur and the Word," "Immigration of the Bodysnatchers," "Walking Philosophy," "Progress of Myth in East Haddam"; *Partisan Review:* "At the Other End of the Telescope"; *Poetry:* "Some Assembly Required," "For the New Ark"; *Southwest Review:* "The World Put Back Together."

"In an Old Garden" also appeared in *The Best American Poetry, 1998* (Scribners), edited by John Hollander and David Lehman. "The U.S.A. Today," "Apologia," and "My Poem Meets Tamerlane" first appeared in *Bright Pages,* an anthology edited by J. D. McClatchy for Yale University Press.

Library of Congress Cataloging-in-Publication Data
Bradley, George, [date]
    Some assembly required : poems / by George Bradley.
      p. cm.
    ISBN 0-375-41195-X
     I. Title.
  PS3552.R227 S66 2001
  811'.54—dc21   2001032667

Manufactured in the United States of America
Published August 16, 2001
Second Printing, December 2001

Contents

II

I

The Aerie

My East End home was homeland to the wind,
A source of steady, inexpensive power
We harnessed with a louvered wheel linch-pinned
To gears atop a galvanized steel tower,
Flatland aerie for a nest of owls.
A child gone forth, at dusk I'd climb a tree
And watch the raptors float hair-raising vowels
To startle prey beneath my canopy. . . .
Since then, the copse is cut, the house is sold,
The vanes have fallen from the unused mill,
And all the birds are flown, but I can still
(Whenever memory's twilight falls on me)
Ascend into that blood-red sky and see
The shadows stir, the waiting wings unfold.

Autochthons Are Standing By

What he was was neither more nor less, even
If the dismayed faces assisting at the accident
Of his occurrence theorized as much, improvised
That answer to the anomaly of their distress,
If their eyes grown wide as orbs of herbivores
Searched his for freak flamboyance, dread device,
For thunder stones, dark stars, the attar of all rose,
Raging rivers where he rippled with restraint;
Not more, and yet not less, no incompetent of fact,
Whinging pup, pubescent klutz, no nubile maid
Ablush with tenderness and embarrassment of thought;
Who stepped out, too, through the entanglements
Of day, who apprehended also the swift approach
Of spangled night, as much as they or any tree
He was no more or less than of this earth,
Hallowing its dead, grateful for its bread, bred
Just as they were up to his earth's appointed task—
The analysis of portions of the universal light,
The asking shadows out of it to sorcer and so tell
Of project turned tumulus, habitation left in flame,
Of weary roads and years and the persistent syllables
Still struggling toward this moment, unto its indigenes,
That the accumulated wisdom find them out as well,
The charred words on their lips catch fire again and live.

A Poet in the Kitchen

West Fifty-third was still Hell's Kitchen
the summer I first came to town,
Eleventh Avenue was boarded up,
the West Side Drive was falling down;
Jimmy Carter was still President,
though he'd become a running joke;
Abe Beame had recently been Mayor,
and New York City was flat broke.
I, too, was broke, the flat was free,
and so I landed in that place,
a walk-up three-room shotgun which
a gallery used for storage space
and where I could stay as long as I liked,
provided I kept an eye on the art . . .
but truth be told, it was hard to tell
where art might end and garbage start.
The premises hadn't been cleaned in years,
and clarity was not what the art was about—
there was clutter right up to the ceiling,
and I didn't dare throw anything out.
The bowl of cornflakes off in a corner,
the wall stuck here and there with pins,
might be a mural by Dike Blair
or an "installation" of Mel Chin's;
ink spilled across some binder paper,
pencil hashmarks by the phone,
might be a Vollmer, or a Tuttle,
or just a doodle by no one known;
a length of two-by-four was art;
an empty carton was art, too;

so was a hole in the plaster, where
an embalmed cockroach was on view.
There wasn't any inventory
and no way not to be impressed
with the thought that passing judgment
would be trickier than I'd guessed.
The entryway was the room in the back,
where a bathtub clogged the floor,
and a toilet filled an adjacent closet
left unencumbered by a door.
The entrance also served as the kitchen,
with no space, but with a range
on which I cooked whatever fare
I'd scraped together with spare change:
mashed potatoes drowned in ketchup,
kidney beans boiled in the can,
onions, pizza crust, and lettuce
chopped up with Crisco in a pan.
The middle room, which had no windows,
held a mattress, though no bed,
and what I hoped were only scattered
books I took a chance and read.
The room up front looked out on a lot,
and I used to sit for hours and stare
at days of 1979
from a Day-Glo painted chair,
contemplating a state of affairs
that appeared to be falling apart,
acquiring the taste for odd interiors
it takes to dwell in the House of Art.

I see myself then, learning to view
this world with a noncommittal eye:
the Russians are in Afghanistan,
stagflation is at an all-time high;
outside, the Iranian revolution
is in its first chaotic year;
inside, a poet's in the kitchen
washing won-tons down with beer.

Some Assembly Required

Stand in line at the SuperSave, and it all falls
Into place, Princess Di and the aliens and diet
Tips from outer space, King Tut and King Elvis,
    Out of the subfusc air, the rank urgency of dusk,
    Among the heavy odors of differing dungs,
    Acrid signatures of urine, the bold perfume of musk . . .
Nostradamus, this year's Senate race, unforeseen
Links between absolutely everything and sex,
Conspiracies requiring conspiracy to be detected,
    From a sibilance of scattered leaves, the sudden
    Snap of twig, inflections of a gabbling breeze,
    Horizons stained with dust, the attitude of trees . . .
And O my fellow shoppers waiting to check out,
What appetite is this that drives such dim belief,
What thirst for intercourse between these banal bits?
    From the cacophony of birds as from abrupt silence,
    Odd sounds of usual insects, subliminal presence
    Of added shadow, faintest trembling in the ground . . .
When greed and accident stand ever ready to explain,
Whence this convolvulus of tenuous connection?
What need for the devious when the obvious will do?
    From remarkable weeds, from a slight imbalance
    In the normal proportion of game, from distressed bark,
    Out of the bewildering swirl of importunate sense . . .
Attention, shoppers, there lies a veldt within us each,
Its grasses rustle with intent, and on that plain
Was born the fine suspicion that has carried us so far,

To behold the unassuming fact and comprehend design,
To look upon confusion and construct its plot and act,
To leap at merest notion found floating in the mind . . .
Has brought us to these sheltered aisles under thin gray light,
Where in boredom and abundance we seek our narrative,
Whatever tale comes now to kill us and can creep.

Geistesblitz

It came quietly, unexpected and entire,
Came without wings and echoed by no hymn
(Airy appraisal having risen from earth,
Eccentric beasts retired to their perfection),
That there would be no choosing, not by you
Or any other, no call to heed, no response,
For fatal accident had already been.
It came to you one evening, regarding winter's
Trash, at the muddy edge of a windswept river
Where ice-filled ruts flashed like broken glass,
Came hushed as gentle wavelets lapping, came
Without heat in no flames but setting sun,
That this scene, too, was essential of the past,
That this place, also, was instinct with future,
That a grim wisdom remained anxious to be told,
And wanting others, the teller must be you.
There was no gesture in that light, no voice
Beyond wind's pitch and water's sly percussion,
And yet the matter came to mind as spirit
Slips into a room, as clouds move, stealthy fact:
That those adequate of speech were timid
Of the task, those willing of the effort all
Ill-prepared to speak, that still this river
Moved and anyway would have its say.
And you saw it was the same river, compulsion
Incomplete and unoriginal, a currency
Whose passage was the permanence allowed;
Saw people were what they had always been,
Faithless, distracted, already ghosts on its shore;
Saw in the instant's penetration that the scribe

Is always found, involuntary and without
Discretion, one by the water who must heed
Insinuations of its sound, must gaze
Upon its motion, ingest its unrolled scroll
(That flowing glagolitic script), the one
Available, necessary and therefore apt
To grasp revelation out of a river's flux
(That each life is apocalypse writ small,
That no devastation ever makes an end),
To hear its scaly choir, set its fish to dance,
Insist its serpents sing their songs again.

At the Other End of the Telescope

the people are very small and shrink,
dwarves on the way to netsuke hell
bound for a flea circus in full
retreat toward subatomic particles—
  difficult to keep in focus, the figures
at that end are nearly indistinguishable,
generals at the heads of minute armies
differing little from fishwives,
emperors the same as eskimos
huddled under improvisations of snow—
  eskimos, though, now have the advantage,
for it seems to be freezing there, a climate
which might explain the population's
outré dress, their period costumes
of felt and silk and eiderdown,
their fur concoctions stuffed with straw
held in place with flexible strips of bark,
and all to no avail, the midgets forever
stamping their matchstick feet,
blowing on the numb flagella of their fingers—
  but wait, bring a light, clean the lens . . .
can it be those shivering arms are waving,
are trying to attract attention, hailing you?
seen from the other end of the telescope,
your eye must appear enormous,
must fill the sky like a sun,
and as you occupy their tiny heads
naturally they wish to communicate,
to tell you of their diminishing perspective—
  yes, look again, their hands are cupped

around the pinholes of their mouths,
their faces are swollen, red with effort;
why, they're screaming fit to burst,
though what they say is anybody's guess,
it is next to impossible to hear them,
and most of them speak languages
for which no Rosetta stone can be found—
    but listen harder, use your imagination . . .
the people at the other end of the telescope,
are they trying to tell you their names?
yes, surely that must be it, their names
and those of those they love, and possibly
something else, some of them . . . listen . . .
the largest are struggling to explain
what befell them, how it happened
that they woke one morning as if adrift,
their moorings cut in the night,
and were swept out over the horizon,
borne on an ebbing tide and soon
to be discernible only as distance,
collapsed into mirage, made to become
legendary creatures now off every map.

Nabu-Kudurri-Usur and the Word

Nothing of the sort occurred, of course,
not the evil dreams, not the dementia,
neither bovine diet nor bestial appearance,
hair like feathers, nails like claws of birds;
it hadn't happened that way at all, as any
number of high officials with impeccable credentials
would surely have testified, had they been asked.
When the great king Nabu-Protects-the-Dynasty—
who had driven Pharaoh from the land,
who impressed the might of Marduk upon all nations,
who restored the ziggurats, constructed city walls,
and built the Pensile Paradise for no more
than a woman's delectation—
lay down to end his days,
favored concubines bathed the fevered brow,
musicians played quietly at a distance, and priests
intoned the rituals in reverential whispers.
Costly medicine was brought in from afar,
astronomagi were commanded to hazard an opinion,
and the king—might he live forever!—expired
in the complete possession of majesty, attended
by comely eunuchs and wrapped in rich tradition;
and if it is true that bribed bodyguards
and a perfumed pillow assisted to that end,
that, too, was ancient practice and not undignified,
nothing like the lies contemptible slaves would spread.
But those self-mutilating eaters of insects
who lived in mud huts by stagnant ditches,
who had seen the temple of their god destroyed,
their city walls dissected stone from stone,

their citizens dragged off in chains
by a king whose name they garbled: *Nebuchadnezzar*—
those human trophies of a minor campaign
composed events to their entire satisfaction,
impressing clay with preposterous inventions,
relentlessly recensing their unlikely tales until
they had perfected phrase, reformed the facts,
and then the king abandoned faith with reason,
then the lord of waterways knelt down in the fields
to accept the dew-wet grass into his ox-wide mouth,
brought under the humiliating yoke of madness
by a pitiless investment, by that unconscionable thing,
the right word released upon this feckless world.

Zen of the Great Dismal Swamp

Neck-deep in the *palus* of particulars—
Thrust in fecundity and rot, the liquefaction
Of flesh animal and vegetable, all but submerged
In spasm, the start of prey from inevitable attack,
In frenzy, opposed imperatives of lust and fear,
Inside the kaleidoscopic vision of repetitious fact—
Denizens, clutched by weedy circumstance, must tread
Muck furiously simply to survive and so rarely
Manage breaching or the great leap vigorous
Enough to comprehend the nature of their confine,
Behold its great extent, define their site sufficiently
To perceive the not unshapely state they're in. . . .

We try. Long ago and far away, a prince
Dressed as a beggar sat beneath a tree until
The cyclic seamlessness around him seemed
Distant as the sun, detached more than the moon,
So removed as to be beautiful, a blaze of light and love.
In that instant the prince smiled and became
A god, became a statue and the statue's story
And ceased all other manner of becoming.
Meanwhile, outside the palace where the prince
Had left behind particulars of wife and child,
The diseased creatures whose mere existence
Had provoked long search and great revelation
Shifted on the marble, scratched persistent sores,
Peered each in his cup to count the blessings of that day.

Immigration of the Bodysnatchers

They arrived and were so beautiful, it was sad
They refused to snatch you, too, the aliens.
Teenage warriors resplendent in their fatigues,

Callow refugees of a conflict not given you
To understand, replete though it ever be
With disputed borders and the requisite enmities,

With the usual appalling blood-letting
And inadequate measures of relief,
They appeared in your home town

And signed on for the next campaign.
Nonchalant tacticians, plugged in to the mumble
Of a culture between languages and rapt

In the comparison of monochrome tattoos,
They wound up by surrounding you
Without paying much attention, although

They paused now and then to glance your way
And sometimes mingled indifference with your need.
It was touching, of course, and annoying

And soon over, for now they must move on again
To their idea of love, grunting and gesticulating,
Cunning in their not quite random remarks—

Protective coloration for a forest in which you
Find no repast—and so carry the sprawl forward
In all its ripeness and decay, slick under its sun,

Bound for that pitiless display of affection
That will clutch them by and by as the centaur's
Bloodstained cloak, but which for the nonce

Dawns as a splendor they alone decode
Gazing into glory holes, the abundant fire
And animal glitter of one another's eyes.

The U.S.A. Today

Homespun sang-froid composed of kaffeeklatsch,
The calm was as persistent as crab-grass,
And one witnessed hardly any gnashing of teeth,
The ritual breast-beating and rending of garments
Effectively preempted by trips to the hardware store
And close inspection of box scores in the sports pages,
By annual drives for the American Cancer Society
And endless discussion concerning inconsequential variations in
 the ongoing entertainment of weather.
So the city fathers sent out the fire engines to process,
And an ironclad normality prevailed, though if this
Be courage or stupidity, boredom or despair,
Remained hidden even from themselves,
Good citizens practicing the standard necromancies
And battening on their own ambition,
Who in sunlight ripened a rictal grin
And by night admitted into dreams
The children they had been
To stand whimpering by the side of the bed
While the gold threads were torn out of their scalps,
Their rosy complexions once more drained of blood,
The thin limbs hacked from their hairless bodies
And buried in separate boxes before dawn,
That renewed adults, awaking to the vision
Of an order still to be delivered, might hunger
For the shewbread of astonishment and pick up
The drive-thru punishment of one day's understanding.

Experiments in Creation Science

He went in through the top and extracted information at random:
    names of childhood friends, how to factor equations, dates of
    battle, objects to be bought, words, appointments, promises,
    items for immediate action, food for further thought.
He carved away flesh with a jagged chisel and replaced
    musculature with mush; what was left resembled a boiled
    chicken left on a rack to dry.
He poured gravel into articulations and wound springy step tight.
He dispersed the enticing aura of pheromones and added an acrid
    whiff of fear, a fetor of adrenaline, indelible odors of
    compound distress.
He lengthened distance, blurred detail, reduced sound to faintest
    rumor; the walk along the shore became a marathon on ice.
He contributed ache and heartache, turning bliss to remembrance.
He besieged ambition and injected doubt; each hour arrived to
    portion out defeat.
He increased wisdom, and tears ran; a sigh insinuated itself,
    creeping forward into laughter.
He compressed the whole and bent it.
He draped it on any available support.
He regarded the result and decided to start over.
His spirit moved on the face of the deep, and there was morning,
    there was evening, and that was another day.

For the New Ark

Cockroaches, of course, the professionals,
As well as most varieties of lice,
And indeed insects of every description,
The crawlers, slitherers, drillers, hoppers, and fliers,
The gulpers, siphoners, champers, lappers, and munchers;
A quantity of rodents, and particularly rats,
Their red-rimmed, malevolent eyes glowing
From behind nibbled sacks of grain;
Deer, against odds, and many domesticated ungulates,
Their capacity to provide for others and absorb abuse
Come at this crux to their aid;
No frogs, no turtles, no elephants, and very few fish;
Dizzying numbers of microbes, the mutable;
Pigeons, scavengers par excellence,
And such birds as dispose of much carrion,
But no songbirds, and nothing of startling plumage;
No rhinoceroses, clearly, or pandas, and nothing like a whale;
Surprisingly few lizards;
No coral;
No marsupials except the opossum,
Yet raccoons, boars, and several bears;
Jellyfish;
Dogs, cats, worms, the more circumspect of arachnids . . .
These the companions fit and unfit for Man,
Who sets out today upon the ocean of hereafter,
Equipped with the vague notion of arrival
And his idea of deity, ark of quaint construction,
To bob upon the deep until

The inundation of hours shall drain away
As his heart's thought shall recede, leaving
The fugue of light, leaping and releaping off of water,
Leaving that general dank giving of the past,
Its bloated scatterings, its layered silt,
And also the cartilaginous invertebrates,
And those parasites salvaged within the vessel of their host.

Spagyric

It got on mountains and they crumbled, the marl washing from
    their spines, their rock turned talus slope.
It touched seas and they shrank. Their harbors silted up, their
    mud petrified to slate.
It got on deserts and they gained arroyos, meadows and they knew
    no grass again.
It got on graves and the epitaphs rinsed clean.
It weighted every movement.
It rode each beam of light.
It got on memories and they warped, approximating negatives of
    the pain that had occasioned them.
Faces thrust into it melted, tallow to its eternal flame.
Wood it fingered spalded, checked.
Metal it found rust bit hard.
It laminated cities. Buildings it brushed fell down, glass littering
    piazzas while intricate brickwork unzipped.
It got on gods and they were superstition.
It got on facts and they became the name of ignorance. Branches
    of science withered, academies were closed.
Words could not evade it. They were deprived of context.
Planets could not avoid it. Wobbling, they cooled.
Its wind reached for the stars, and stars flickered out.
It got on poems. The poems exploded, becoming scraps of
    misconstruction.
It got on those flinders also, that thus assumed a shape, that
    settled into evidence, the difference we see—clunch
    topography of chert degree.
Its solvent bathes all objects, discovering the density of each.
In its wake lies sheer resistance, the spew of what is stubborn.
    Wrecked recalcitrance. This strewn obtuse.

Sorrow's Season

In time of sorrow, do not speak.
Let the wind speak,
that has seen everything,
that remembers nothing,
its cry always
the sound of its own passage.

In time of sorrow, listen to the sea,
that grumbles at its limits,
that ruminates and ruminates
and is not satisfied until
the gristle of its argument
be ground down in fine.

In sorrow lies the time to mark
that other ocean, earth,
that accepts much,
that yields little,
keeping secrets with its peace
as vast tides turn and slow waves roll.

Though air explode in empty rage,
though waters churn in frenzy,
pressure build within the soil
and locked plates shudder,
fabrication fall,
yet sorrowing behold them all,

for sorrow's season is meet for witness,
and this the only world we have,
that clamors, that abides.
We must invent some other world
before the spirit of election shifts
again in us to sing.

Walking Philosophy

There are worlds, unwieldy, dreadful,
Difficult to grasp, just pick one up
And it grasps you, its grip of iron;

And there are sights, brochure-loads,
Wonders ancient and otherwise, but look
Too close and blur becomes confusion;

People, and they shrink from cultivation,
Beat retreats; facts, and the more you know
Of each the less you'll want to hang

On any, comes time for feet to dangle in the sky
While windswept clouds make blotchy patterns,
Gussy up some valley floor many feet below . . .

Patterns, yes, and the multiples thereof,
But they must come to you, haply
As rays picking up earth's gravitation,

Must find you staring into space, puttering
In the yard, out walking, aimless and amazed.
The unwasted life has not been lived.

The World Put Back Together

To climb a tree and shout up at the sun,
To run for pleasure dancing in a ring,
To offer questions old since time began
Yet new to you—what's that but to be young
And sensitive to that entrancing tune
We all have heard but few remember long?
So poets write at first out of their talent
Who often in an awkward age fall silent.

A child of ten is still a perfect creature,
Sure of its affections, quick to form
New views, being on easy terms with Nature,
That never yet has done it any harm;
But soon, with adolescence for a teacher,
It's put to trade, to watch with mute alarm
The world its parents gave it on a platter
Whirl away and like a dropped toy shatter.

That plaything broken, unearned wisdom once
Undone is weary labor to refashion,
For to be wise, whatever else it means,
Implies a mortal struggle with confusion;
And as a man struck blind must learn the sense
Of touch, now having lost the trick of vision,
Youth must sift the fragments of its soul
And from them try to cobble up the whole.

And I, who have arrived at forty-three,
Am made to face anew this childish task,
To reinvent my world in poetry

By sorting through its pieces dawn to dusk,
While what had seemed an innate fluency
Becomes a quarrel cluttering my desk,
The stammered happiness, the clotted rage . . .
A sought composure, page on crumpled page.

What if the shape I make's mere ornament,
A heap collected out of bits that glitter?
What if its peace is never permanent:
I turn my back, it runs away like water?
Sheer fascination and the effort spent
Can't make a bitter question taste the sweeter;
What of that? The dream this world coheres
Is old as Man and music to my ears.

My Poem Meets Tamerlane

Many things happen in Chester, Connecticut,
but the invasion of Tamerlane is not one of them.
Instead, the streets are plowed and the buses run,
my Mr. Coffee radio-alarm swings into action,
and I'm just wondering if a sense of civic responsibility
isn't the instinct to mediocrity, when another account
of the cosmos gets tossed on my porch, containing
A) nothing whatsoever about my poetry, and B)
such shenanigans that I conclude the notion
of civic responsibility is a thing of the past, until
I notice an item about bloodshed in the Caucasus
(the Congo, the Murex Coast, the Transoxiana),
where vengeance remains the one idea and starvation
sinks its fangs into the blown bellies of children
as it has since Man knoweth not to the contrary
(dust is rising off the steppe, say, in A.D. 1395,
and the far cry of trumpets forecasts extinction;
as my poem is invested by Tamerlane, fear
sweeps its populace as the dawn wind sweeps water),
meaning a passable ennui is not short of perfection,
i.e., if the urge to eminence accomplishes such havoc
surely we need always all the mediocrity we can get.
Then who am I to complain of disregard
when all history comes to an unmarked grave,
when obscurity lies in ambush at each road's end,
when earth is a mother with a dead thing at her breast?
Who shall record the myriad configurations of pain?
And what is to tell but of hope gone under the ground?

Friend, Tamerlane the Great rides this and every day,
and the corpses stretch to infinity behind him.
They must rot where they fall. And I sing one life,
I find joy and the prospect of peace. Sing not
and my bones have already been scattered.

Carmen and Error

How sad that there should be so many
never to see Carmen dance, to observe
the silk illusion she spun round herself,
to watch her body freeze against the light,
so many not to hear her song, to sense
the quick click of her castanets,
to attend the ecstasy and grief
in the cry torn from her throat,
its wild accord to music played
in patterns old as thought.
That so much passion be spent
on an eternal few!—for an aging waiter,
the usual shepherds, the whore
of a one-whore town, plus the odd
tourist arrived with a tattered guide
to the curiously cunning and quaint.
A shame, those steps should stir
no multitude, that ululation rise
as silence, pitiful, and worse,
in this how not to feel a judgment,
a condemnation much unwitnessed,
yet condemnation all the same?
Surely it was feeble song that drew
but faint response, awkward dance
that could not crowd a room,
for all the crowd was uninstructed,
the room as vast as space and time.
And if the crowd was the thing it was,
what might change except the song?
It was melody must find the audience,

the dancing make its motion known,
must start tonight from this day's village
and find its road to the end of the earth.

But such talk left Carmen unimpressed,
who loved her song and her way with it
and nothing that did not lend its ear.
Carmen spat and said it was her dance
had cleft this world in two—those
happy enough to witness it, those
dull enough to be untouched—and they
that never knew must thereby plague
another place, condemned to suffer
elsewhere for an error all their own,
exiled to an inferior condition, forced
in ignorance to distract themselves,
say in Kazakhstan, at some last resort
on the dregs of the Aral Sea,
where untrained lifeguards dressed
in hides and carried truncheons,
and a faint odor of burning dog
carried all the way from Tashkent.

Apologia

If our ears were not pavilions of desire,
Bright canopies, billows pitched and spread,
Painted sails upon the restless main of thought;
If they were not gardens, damp enclosures thick
With fruit and vivid bloom, not winding palaces,
Not rococo cathedrals and frivolous gazebos
And castles of caprice, eccentric merlons perched
In architectural defiance upon the wildest crag,
Then—O Acting Assistant to an Acting Editor—
We might oblige remark, hark as you would hear.

And if our speech were not another dialect,
Our own rude gutturals, our sympathetic clicks,
The odd stress and persistent superfluous schwa;
If our words weren't cultivations and gibberish
To that communal, quick, quotidian chameleon
That darts and squeaks, vigorous on its twig,
Then—O Interim Director of an Underfunded Series—
We might state your case and say your grace,
Offer up the bread that mumbles on your plate.

And further, if fierce rapidity weren't in the air,
This violent mistral, this manic will to change
That rips the sound out of our mouths and steals
Our *sfumature*, a turbulent simoom of difference
Withering pun to explanation, the surreptitious
To blank stare; if the tramontana of mutation
Were not always at our throats, why then—

O Temporary Muck-a-Muck of the Edifice on Paper—
Then we might deal plainly with plain truths,
Simply say what soothes, might seek and suffer
Little clarity, accept the sentence of the meek.

But Muck-a-Muck, our ears are shameless, self-indulged;
Our words remain our intimates and the paraphrase
Of dream, melodies that echo down enchanted corridors;
And the wind that howls above this house tonight
Sweeps our idea away like leaves torn from the trees.
Who will be left to satisfy but us and what is not?
We testify at other hearings, before a terrible tribunal
Of flimsy things: the model irony of strangers,
The enthused naifs of day, the unresponsive innocence
Pressed to remove us and be all we have been.

Treppwörter

As the last reveler descending from the feast
Grips the marble balustrade and hears
(The caress of conversation over now,
The clink of spoon on stemware at an end,
The punch lines told, the healths all drunk,
The few prepared remarks dutifully applauded,
And musicians hired to play old favorites
Gone off to improvise in jazz clubs until dawn)
The evening's facund repartee once more
Wing its way across a crowded room, and as
On entering the unconvivial street below
He knows too late the words one might have said,
So I, the accents echoing in my head
Of departed voices that will not wait
Upon our answer or concern themselves
With our affairs, address my discourse
To the dead and find my thought in theirs
And know that insofar as art is wit
Its wit is of the stairs.

A Year in New England

CHRISTMAS STORM DOWN EAST

Over the Mini-Mart *cum* filling station;
Over the package store that was a bank
Till banks lost interest in the situation;
Over track still racing to outflank
Wetlands no one bothers to reclaim;
Over the collapsed expansion-tank
Beside the empty factory that became
An empty theater; over gentle peaks
In an economy (if that's the name),
Based on tag sales, ammo, and antiques,
Along with bookstores not to be discussed
And the volumes that such silence speaks;
Over a new world asked to readjust,
Snow comes down miraculous as dust.

FIRST LIGHT

No traffic on the road as morning breaks;
No squirrels on the roof; why, even crows,
Those bumptious birds, are quiet when it snows:
Listening in your bed, you feel the flakes
Of calm accumulate within your head
To insulate the world from its alarms,
To stall commuters, mute the call to arms
Of tooth and claw, and let you snooze instead . . .
And then it comes, at first so lost in distance
Its tremble might be nothing but temblor,
But building to a rumble, then a roar,
Till sowing salt and shattering resistance,
Rattling the groggiest enthusiast
Of sleeping in, the plow's huge blade sweeps past.

HOUSEGUEST

In winter, when calamities environ
The coziest of homes—a river frozen
Stiff across its current, temperatures
Of ten below, and earth like sculpted iron—
No known deterrent can prevent a house
From taking in the tenant who prefers
Whatever perfidy his hosts have chosen
To fields off-putting to a mortal mouse.
The steel wool packed in each inviting nook,
The trap demurely set, the poison out . . .
Regardless, one poor boarder, bent by hook
Or crook to prove foundations badly built,
Will come to scamper through the walls like doubt
And even if suppressed will stink like guilt.

MUD SEASON

It's all the ground can do to hold the past
In place. Just scratch the surface anywhere
With tractor tread, the print of boot or paw,
Scattered branches shed by timber freighted
With wet snow and ceaselessly harassed
By wind, and should the soil meet open air
As mud, the objects sticking in its craw
Can't be kept down and are regurgitated:
Plastic and glass, plutonic rock that last
Saw light an Ice Age since, what bone can bear
The paroxysm that is frost and thaw
Intact . . . the man-made and/or carbon-dated
Data someone buried to forget
Dredged up from earth's oozy oubliette.

MILLRACE

Each April's different: this one saw a spate
Of rain increase the run-off from the snow
To make the village millpond overflow
Well-groomed banks and leap an unused gate
Into the race, which had not felt the flood
In fifty years. That's when the mill and wheel,
Back then thought insufficiently genteel,
Were leveled and the stream shut up for good,
Or so it seemed. But flood will out, commotion
Run its course. I watched the water boil
Through undergrowth, sluicing astonished soil
Off toward the deep disturbance of our ocean,
And so subside and next day leave no trace
But mud and some erosion in the race.

A SCRAP OF SKY

The bluebird, famous for the scrap of sky
Borne on his back—an indigo so bright
That just a glimpse of his distinctive flight,
All swoop and flurry, captivates the eye
And makes us smile for having made us start—
Has hope and optimism to the marrow,
Or has at least the pluck to reappear
In fields where he was dispossessed last year;
And there that feathered terrier the sparrow,
Bearing no more than murder in his heart,
Will once more wait to steal the nest and drive
The weaker, more attractive bird away.
So beauty comes each spring and tries to stay,
And so does drab determination thrive.

FLY DOPE

Because a store-bought bugspray meets its match
Faced with backwoods when the blackflies hatch,
You'll want thick clothing soaked in creosote,
Not forgetting netted hat and gloves,
To hold off hungry mandibles that float
Through June in indefatigable droves.

What might it signify that superficies
Be so besieged, if surface form a gauge
Of rudimentary fact? This is the Age
Of Insects—we can't even count their species—
And it's our sense of self that is assailed.
Man's dominion had its place in theory.
Cognition is an evolutionary
Experiment that has already failed.

A DIAGNOSIS

You say your summer limp does not improve,
Joints ache daily and the night sweats linger,
Your stomach heaves if you but lift a finger,
Your head spins at the notion you might move?
Then—since you have cancer at the least,
Probably dengue fever, river blindness—
Beseech a friend to shoot you out of kindness;
Unless, of course, you live in the northeast
United States, in which case you have Lyme
Disease and have a healthy chance to beat
What is a tick-transmitted spirochete
That mingled with your blood in some sublime
Moment indulged with that great Avatar
Whose favored child and chosen prey you are.

CANICULAR

Hard, cicada quaver in crescendo
And sunlight's throb a headache overhead,
To miss the season's earthy innuendo
Apropos the rumpled flower bed;
And difficult, as desiccation stains
The lawn and wrinkles liver-spotted leaves,
To be a spirit ripeness entertains
Or whom a breath of evening air deceives
With memories of how the iris blade
Thrust through mulch as if to reach the stars
And raised a sea-green spar that soon displayed
Blue flag buds wrapped tightly as cigars;
It was their wattles, draped and shriveling,
That hung the crepe upon the rites of spring.

PRAYER UPON DEPARTURE

Absorbed in late September's oblique rays
And soon to be the plaything of thin air,
The Monarch of whatever he surveys
Clasps dalmatic wings as if in prayer,
Instinctively invoking aid, perhaps,
Before migration of two thousand miles.
Meanwhile, a decayed world becomes an apse-
Mosaic, blades and leaves enameled tiles
Placed at ideal angle to the light
And shimmering as wind begins to rise.
Wings stir and pause. The season's cloisonné
Glints. The butterfly seems poised for flight.
We have to love what bears us on our way
Or be unbearable in our own eyes.

PROGRESS OF MYTH AT EAST HADDAM

Like doe-skin mittens, mottled marigold
And pinned up by the roadside on display,
Trembling hands the silver birches hold
Applaud the denouement of autumn day;
Like light shed from a Gothic altarpiece,
Gold leaf streaked with scarlet underpaint,
The maples' glory is their own release,
A martyrdom tricked out to tempt a saint;
Like battered bindings of maroon morocco,
Like remnants of antique upholsteries,
Like flutterings of copper birds that flock to
Leave, the brightness falling from the trees
Reminds us that our world is metaphor:
A Golden Age will pass us by once more.

IN AN OLD GARDEN

Some cloudy, colorless November day,
When leaves are down and odd uneven gray
Lines show up where recently a lush
Wall of impenetrable underbrush
Obscured all sign of such impediments
As constitute a fieldstone garden fence,
With autumn over, winter unarrived,
You stumble on whatever has survived
Of old New England farms: the border cairns
That mark an orchard gone to woods; a barn's
Mere outline; perhaps a hollow to surprise
The foot, telling how wells internalize
Themselves; and—look!—one sky-blue cupid's dart
That given time will learn its rime by heart.

THE GIFT

for Spencer Boyd

All night, as we lay sleeping, frozen rain
Has coated our community: the crimson
Maple spread above our eaves, the plane
Tree that adorns our boundary line, the Jimson
Weed and wandering Jew (what's left of such
In such a season, tattered etamines
Discarded near a garden wall or hutch),
And hardy, no, foolhardy evergreens
That can't bear to refuse these dangerous gifts,
And so at dawn are jeweled and glitter-gowned
And greet the extraordinary light that lifts
Both great and small (or all the thaw has found
Unbroken by bequest, unbowed by years)
With rising boughs and bright, persistent tears.

II

How I Got in the Business

Finding yourself in the olive oil line
  is not like becoming a poet:
mothers don't burst into tears at the news,
  and fathers don't hide behind newsprint,
muttering something about needing now
  to plan for a triple retirement.
Quite the contrary, family desires
  are usually how people get started
(well, of course, but I mean in the trade).
  your uncle, let's say, is a prominent
mafia boss who cornered the oil
  imported from Campobasso,
but who neglected to get his degree
  and so buys your way into Harvard,
where it will be your privilege to see
  the best minds of a generation
sitting in traffic on Memorial Drive,
  befriending the exiled Caribbean
dictators who frequent the Kennedy School
  of Government, and waiting on endless
queues for fancy ice cream in the snow.
  You're there to learn accounting,
how to amortize armor in limousines,
  but one day crossing Plympton,
pausing by chance, you glance in the glass
  of what is an overstuffed closet
known as the Grolier Book Shop and find
  there's no accounting (or even
shame) where poetry's taste is concerned,
  and seduced by such revelation

you yield body and soul to the urge
   to attract the notice of critics,
aching to pass for a poet of parts.
   You've purchased the clothing-as-attitude
needed and wangled permission to take
   the celebrity poet seminar,
when—tipped off by the brutes he assigned
   to cover your backside in Cambridge—
suddenly Uncle gets wind of what's up,
   and next thing you know you're shoveling
chickenshit under an olive tree, sent
   for your sins and further instruction
back to the fields of your ancestral home
   in the hardscrabble hills of Trinacria,
there to outgrow poetic conceits
   by gleaning proverbial wisdom
dropped from the mouth of a toothless *paesan*
   (*un uomo, i calzoni di nuovo*
su, non sta in pensiero piu)
   and so to learn something useful,
starting in oil from the terrain up.
   That's one way, a perfectly good way,
not that it's mine, to find yourself
   in the business. And maybe years later,
after you know all that one can
   about guano, why a sack of *pollina*
isn't so cheap as it seems (it's rich
   in nitrogen but dissolves so slowly
you'll be forced to use twice as much
   as you would with what are apparently

more expensive artificial manures);
  long after, perhaps, when smuggling
in second-rate product from Spain
  to pass off as yours no longer
offers mystery, and the chemistry used
  in lowering acidity and altering
color has been fully absorbed and applied;
  when the right combination of bribery,
threat, and persistence (which is what it takes
  to pacify pruners and pickers,
coddle bureaucrats in D.C. and Rome,
  and intimidate the Greek immigrant
owners of pizzerias from Miami to Nome)
  comes naturally to you as breathing;
decades later, when you're adept
  at extracting a profit from the scenery,
coaxing it off of contorted trees
  and persuading it into a bottle,
out of a warehouse, and onto a shelf;
  when deceptive labeling's your art form;
when you could write the definitive book
  on fraudulent government subsidies;
when the remaining hurdle you face
  is finding compliant accountants;
possibly *then* you will come back to verse,
  your object of first affectation,
brought there by boredom and a newspaper ad.
  One evening at home in Jersey,
scanning the *Times* alongside a wife
  inspiring no poetry, you notice

notices for venues of verse in New York,
  among them a cultured gymnasium
sporting the name "The 92nd St. Y"
  and touting a suitably strenuous
schedule of readings, and by gum you go.
  The choice was either television
personalities celebrating a poet's demise
  or a highly professional expatriate
said to be reading in Polish, and you opt
  for English, and at long last afterwards,
seriously snarled on the G. W. Bridge
  (by mistake you took the upper
level and forgot to keep to the left),
  you wonder about personalities,
why they insist on affording a poem
  the histrionics of soap opera.
Exiting the mess, you're left with mixed
  emotions (and right there is poetry's
marketing problem), at once confused
  and guilty, because you no longer
like what you thought you loved, because
  the diary entries of others
seem by nature best kept to themselves,
  and when you arrive back in Ridgewood,
you have arrived at contentment, too,
  relieved that you found a vocation
where the restraints to be evaded are clear,
  where mature perspective rarely
asks you to reassess your ideals,
  and where you need never apologize,

caught by a mirror half-way through life,
  to the person you were at age twenty. . . .
That, then, is a typical way into oil,
  although not mine, as I mentioned.
My way, you become a poet first,
  and who could begin to tell you
how such a natural disaster takes place?
  And what makes you think for an instant
mere biography completes the tale?
  Besides, it's hopeless unraveling
all of the strands in that *Bildungsroman,*
  that *Buddenbrooks* thick with collapsing
middle-class circumstance (Thomas Mann
  was right about writing, how it
flourishes in the mulch of bourgeois decay,
  and while the training in hypocrisy
helps—the instinctive grasp of good form
  as something arbitrary by nature—
what's of greater value is the sense
  of nostalgia instilled by declining
fortune, since the author's *sine qua non*
  is memory amplified by wishful
thinking and ready access to books),
  unthreaded labyrinth, backlashed
reel, that steel-belted Gordian knot,
  the tangle of factors hovering
over the page and in each fingertip
  as the oddest kid in the high school
tiptoes down art's primrose path;
  retracing those steps is beyond us,

so we won't bother, aware that the past
  arrives by chance and anyway
poets aren't born, or even made,
  they're stung. It happens you're wading
up to your short hairs in the tropical swamp
  of adolescence, feeling the hormones
frisk, when—ZAP!—you're bit by the bug,
  as fateful to you as Darwin's
contact with the germ of Chagas' disease,
  and you find yourself at that juncture
sentenced for life to evolving dreams,
  a willing host to consuming
fevers the unstung don't know exist,
  become a teen-age ancient
mariner of incomprehensible concern
  and disproportionate project,
all of which is to say that the case
  of the freshman possessed in the bookstore
isn't unusual and might even have worked,
  if only the kid had told Uncle,
cancel the ticket and flat-out forget
  that trip to Palermo, spurning
sight unseen the arena of peaks,
  their impassive audience, wanting
nothing to do with the stingy earth
  behind them, where the olives
straggle across inaccessible slopes
  and the terrible sun of summer
turns the field grass to tinder set
  for the immolation of prospect:

all it takes is lightning to strike,
  and sheets of flame can envelop
whole hectares of ancient estate,
  the oily smoke ascending
hour after hour, as wells are low
  in August and no hydrant's handy.
Unmown groves that catch and burn
  are a warning to all, eyesores
visible far and wide, charred
  and smoldering ruins, a wasteland
such as the would-be poet must make
  of competing deliriums, seeing
sooner or later, no matter how fierce
  or loving the family, you have to
pole-axe their hearts, utterly refuse
  to become the adult they imagined,
need to replace their hope with your own,
  and, turning your back on attachments,
like the young Goethe skating away
  from Mutti toward his *selbstsüchtig*
future, turn into a creature unfit
  for their intentions as for every
other employment, and assuming that you
  have somehow contracted the fever,
too, now what are you going to do?
  You're going to answer to "freelance,"
that's what, working a succession of jobs
  which defy all résumé building:
guarding galleries, delivering food,
  constructing, telemarketing,

standing and also serving (there's
 a waiter in every poet),
sitting babies and houses and pets,
 assisting, flattering, groveling,
actively drifting from this dead end
 to the next, and each day progressing
nowhere, and provided you manage to avoid
 an "entry position" as an escort,
don't complain, because that's the point,
 the best way to wind up a poet
is to resist being anything else,
 which sounds easy but isn't,
no, it's hard to hold out, with hell
 to pay and with opportunity
threatening, but give it a little time,
 and the slough of available drudgery
drains, and you're either a poet or a bum,
 and by then you'll make such distinctions.
Anything you happen to make of yourself
 in the process is optional, though getting
passably versed in verse couldn't hurt:
 you'll find that to spit out a single
poem will entail chewing a lot
 of poems to pieces, a mouthful
yours to bite off, since no one receives
 a foundation breakfast in poetry
these days, when going to graduate school
 is madness and your average professor
sells out of literature to set up in the chic
 arrondissement of critical

theory and its anfractuous, siccative prose.
  Abandoned by high educators,
apt to read up a bit on their own,
  your poets are autodidacts,
always and everywhere and now more
  than ever, their minds irregular
landscapes of panoramic peak
  and appalling abyss, accidents
waiting to happen upon the right word,
  and I have met poets entirely
ignorant of, oh, Foucault who know
  a surprising amount regarding
Byzantine history, or Renaissance art,
  or astronomy, or Mediterranean
agriculture, about olive trees, say,
  the varieties found in an orderly
grove, each with its role, like vines
  in Bordeaux: the *Morolino,*
giving good oil but having small fruit
  and thus a low yield; the *Lecce,*
which is resistant to frost but bland
  in flavor; the *Pendolino,*
named for a drooping habit that weeps
  at the wretched stuff it renders,
planted as a matter of course nonetheless
  for the purpose of cross-pollination,
scattered about amid better trees
  instead of the outmoded *Morchiaio,*
which was used in the old days but throws
  an especially heavy sediment;

finally, there's the *Frantoio,* king
  of the slope, producing an exquisite
oil that's the basis of every fine blend,
  yet a torment to grow, maddening
first on account of its fruit, which matures
  at intervals and so must be harvested
several times at considerable cost,
  and second because it is delicate,
dropping its blossoms at the drop of a hint
  if springtime weather turns chilly,
so that come autumn there's nothing to pick,
  and moreover in danger of freezing
down to the ground in winter, an event
  that decimates hillsides in Italy
every few decades, when truncated boles
  come up from the roots like clustered
spindles, shrubbery too young to yield
  a single olive and with foliage
areas barely adequate to support
  the extensive subterranean
network that fed the departed limbs.
  Reducing a coppice to a coherent
tree is tricky and can't be rushed,
  and it might take all of twenty
years before one hard frost is repaired,
  the way that winnowing saplings
sprung from poetry's taproot down
  to a few careers of significance
waits on the pruning shears of time,
  the aspirant authors dwindling

gradually, first those who can't stand
 rejection, lacking the rhinoceros
hide required to send off new poems
 to *The New Yorker,* there to settle
under a radiator or behind a desk
 till maintenance comes to the editors'
rescue by sweeping them out with the trash;
 and then those acceptance discourages
(meeting success as a poet is like
 encountering failure at anything
else), those daunted by risible sales,
 a skull and crossbones on royalty
statements; and lastly those whom life
 depresses past all prescription,
Zoloft and Paxil and Prozac, and while
 America's an up-to-the-eyebrows
drugged culture, and artists have a right
 to be just as crazy as anybody,
still it seems poems are rarely improved
 by such measures, quite the contrary,
Prozac more often shepherding flocks
 of lines best called Prozaic,
which is why in treating oneself
 for the manic-depressive symptoms
common to poets (to people), I use
 that old-time religion, the mortal
mixture of aspirin, alcohol, and caffeine.
 A deft touch with stimulants has given
wings to many a career, but while
 you're waiting to see if you have it,

don't discount the element of luck,
  and nothing's luckier than randomly
reading and thereby becoming enslaved
  to a stylishly accomplished poet,
preferably one reassuringly dead.
  The object of your veneration
can't be predicted and appears to choose you,
  but once the selection has happened
you will be able to ape to your poems'
  content (copying the eponymous
primate skill and best way to learn),
  and as long as your efforts resemble
others, it means they've no self to be like,
  so you mustn't attempt evasive
action, but rather plow straight ahead,
  producing your votive images
lovingly, lavishly, loyally, until
  at last you are disenchanted,
freed mysteriously as once enthralled,
  released yet defined by the experience,
taking identity, strangest gain,
  away, and that reminds me,
not the least important thing
  you'll learn by imitation is never
be too proud or too stupid to steal,
  for that's what the long shelf is there for,
all those metaphors leaked from the pens
  of poets who thought they were seeking
fame, or maybe the meaning of life,
  but instead were merely reserving

room in the seedy motel of your mind,
  and to quote the apposite idiom,
"same difference." All right, you've dreamt
  the dream with no bottom and awakened
into the glare of its broken spell,
  and how to dispose of such acolyte
ardor? At a loss for mastery, you
  have reached a developmental
moment of risk, faced with a choice,
  a quandary, a puzzle like planting
olives, given that seedlings you strive
  to establish in spring must weather
summer's drought to reach the rain,
  while those held back till autumn
have to survive the winter cold
  before their roots have burrowed
deep enough to be safe, and because
  the wrong decision can wither
promise, consider the lay of the land
  when someone proposes to nurture
talent, ponder the brochure you are sure
  to receive, for, Eager Author,
you'll be the target of junk in the mail
  promoting a poetry conference
set in an obligingly picturesque state
  and featuring a pool, dormitory
dining, a library/video lounge,
  and instruction by Real Writers.
Now, if the writers are rarities who impart
  technique or are connected in publishing,

maybe it's worth the money, since skills
  exist to be learned and acquaintance
raises no obstacle to placing a book;
  more likely, though, you'll meet with
fettered rhyme and frittered time,
  a hellish circuit of abandoned
hopefuls who teach only to avoid
  starvation; and if so, be generous,
dropping a coin in the cup, and get out
  and instead swim off to the biggest
fishpond available, a metropolis where
  you'll camp in that part of the city
currently settled by artists and stand
  in the corners of parties, pretending
not to be feeling too ill at ease,
  until eventually you realize
you are no dumber than everyone else,
  and when the ones standing near you
come to the same conclusion, why that's
  a Movement, a New Generation,
bingo, this is *it,* you've *arrived,*
  your agent is calling to remind you
books you blurb may be your own,
  to mention that fifteen percent of
nothing is nothing, is prose such a crime,
  and say by the way your persona
needs a major makeover, *ciao.*
  Your agent knows the business,
sadly, so now you'll have to decide:
  to self-promote or not bother,

it's a question, if effort and time
  devoted to your reputation
might not better be spent on your poems,
  or if careerism is a separate
craft, the ignoring of which is naive.
  The quantity of energy writers
waste in their burning urge to emit
  the mandorla of success is a caution;
still, if you feel you must join them, you can.
  To make a splash is simple:
just be impossible. From day one
  of kindergarten to the final
scene on an opera stage, if possessed
  of the tiniest bit of ability,
playing the prima donna is the way
  to get that ability noticed
(lift a leaf from an olive, that asks
  for no end of attention, insisting
bags of fertilizer be hauled up hills
  and requiring semiannual
pruning for optimum yield, once
  in winter to remove damaged
wood and improve overall shape,
  and again in summer to eliminate
excess growth, the suckers that sprout
  at the base of each trunk and siphon
nutrients off, if left untrimmed,
  from fruit in the process of ripening):
take my advice and act like a jerk,
  and your clothes will be mentioned in *Vanity*

Fair, your poems featured in *Vogue,*
  you'll be known as an *enfant terrible*
when not plain called a pain in the ass,
  and then one day you'll stumble
on an anthology fifty years old
  and run your eyes over the echoless
names in the table of contents to see
  that while publicity makes every
difference in who gets published today,
  it makes none at all to the remnant
destined to be read tomorrow, and from
  that weedy Gethsemane of versifiers
runs the Via Dolorosa to your art
  and its improvement, though having
disavowed instruction, ditched
  the poetry conference, rejected
seminars and graduate school, you
  are left to your own devices,
cast away on the rocky coast
  of inner resource, and frankly
but for the ploy of reading this poem,
  your posterity's dead on arrival. . . .
Call it your luck, then, and not just
  my own, that by an unprecedented
piece of prosody, the vestigial urge
  to verse, by the miracle of modern
metrics, I'm in the giving vein
  and the mood to chat, the meter's
running but the ride's on me, so find
  a moment's peace and a private

place and feel absolutely free
  to examine this offer at leisure,
weigh each word, consider with care,
  and make my work your workshop.
Now then, five conditions must meet
  and be met in all poems, including
yours: First, it's poetry that shows
  an abandoned love of language,
pleasuring itself with inebriate speech,
  and if you wish to incorporate
words such as *propaedeutic, yark,*
  or *cacozeal* merely to gloppen
readers, why put them in, for verse
  is nothing if not autotelic;
Second, a poem in progress takes pains
  concerning its each enjambment,
otherwise it's no more than prose,
  for lines must be coherent
entities even as stanzas are
  and, as any vessel, shapely;
Third, true poetry must betray
  a metaphysical ambition,
since the art is a religion, and since
  a question chaperoned by answers
doesn't require a second thought,
  much less a second reading;
Fourth, in pursuing its own end,
  a poem must be ambiguous,
which is not the same thing as confused;
  and Fifth, no matter how voluble,

vigorous, or vasty the verse may be,
  a poem must have a conclusion,
not an accident, and enough said.
  And that should get you started,
though as the conditions outlined above
  are necessary, not sufficient,
often your start will be startlingly bad,
  yet do not despair, but remember
Virgil, no less, who is said to have said
  his poems began as inchoate
blobs that had to be licked into shape
  as bear cubs are formed by their mothers,
which illustration, if not the new
  zoology, remains a metaphor
grizzly with unaging intellect when
  it comes to the role of revision,
molder of brightly beslobbered beasts
  and patron saint of poets,
call him San Remedio, invoked
  in the hour of need to polish
erstwhile unreadable verses or put
  them out of their ill-made misery,
mercifully striking what cannot be saved,
  and OK, there you have it,
that's as helpful as I get, and as such
  will have to do and conceivably
might, for wise to the second glance
  that constitutes art's unsettling
gaze, by now you must be prepared—
  ephebe seduced and abandoned,

bit by ambition and stubborn enough
  to persist in ancestral folly—
ready at last for the olive oil trade.
  To tell the truth, you're probably
ready for anything now, who
  have profited little by employment,
labored to acquire no expertise
  beyond an arcane avocation;
lost to the world of sensible work,
  you'll find yourself in pipe dreams
puffed by others, at continual risk
  because you appear to be idle,
staring out windows for much of the day
  with a blank, if not empty, expression,
letting the ideas arrive, an act
  which drives your average relative
batty and leads in-laws to despond
  and so suggest a business
venture involving the FDA,
  for God's sake, and multinational
paperwork, and, Reader, I told them yes,
  and oh, about this idleness
issue—a charge so damning and vague,
  like emotional abuse or latent
racism, that poets will tender claims
  for art's industry and banausic
import in hope they not be condemned
  as superfluous and inherently worthless
drones rather than worker bees,
  those fundamentally American

moral insects—I've heard about
  enough, I don't wish to discuss it,
period, but instead hereby propose
  to do so much to alleviate
human misery in the remaining lines
  of this poem that poets forever
after will be unconditionally absolved
  of a thing so shopworn as utility.
Ready? For canker sores (don't laugh,
  I'm serious; look, living
isn't that different from writing: you solve
  the small problems, since big ones
have to resolve themselves), ignore
  the folk remedy of baking
soda, which saliva soon washes away,
  the pH of the mucous membrane
left unchanged, but rather obtain
  a prescription for silver nitrate,
cauterize each little festering wound,
  and rinse with a good disinfectant.
Your tormented mouth will heal
  by morning, and your temporarily
hobbled speech flow freely again.
  For dandruff, don't listen to hairdressers
pushing pricey medicated shampoos.
  The problem in almost all cases
isn't disease but a dry scalp,
  and too much soap is directly
counterproductive. What you want
  to do is remove the squamous

scurf by massaging with some sort of grit
  (the baking soda you purchased
earlier but didn't use is just
  the thing), and every so often
wash and rinse with a product designed
  to maintain follicle moisture.
Lastly, for piles, you'd better forget
  pomades and pads, which rectify
nothing, and instead send out for ice
  (alas, not to mix cocktails:
alcohol only thins the blood
  and further inflates the swollen
blebs, even as aspirin does)
  to attack the problem directly,
sitting in ice water and holding cubes
  against the offending area.
This will require concentration, but life
  asks courage of us at unlikely
moments, and there is little to gain
  in any pursuit that doesn't
come with its share of discomfort; take
  the gathering of olives, for instance,
which is the last harvest of the year,
  occurring in early December,
after the wind has shifted to the north
  and winter rains begin falling;
nearly frozen, the olives are cold
  as marble chips, the bearing
branches studded with rough twigs,
  and so the pickers must bandage

fingers and wield forceps to strip
  the fruit, collected by preference
slightly shy of ripe, from limbs
  inclined above the stony
slope but disinclined to yield.
  The men and women bringing
in such crops are indigenous as the trees,
  and of course one's called Maria,
dressed in boots and skirt and scarf;
  today—imagine!—is Maria's
final day among these hills
  in which she's spent her seventy
years, for after the harvest she plans
  to live with relatives in the city;
pausing for coffee and a chunk of bread,
  she regards the valley with oval
eyes as lovely, dark and deep
  as olives, and the long perspective
spread before her, which to her mind
  has never seemed so beautiful,
surely will never look the same
  without her, will be missing
something of its sweetness, although
  the haze remain to soften
outlines of all particulars and the hills
  continue their blue recession,
first the ridge with the olive press,
  then farther off the little
town where Maria's *marito* was born,
  then places she has heard of,

never having been, and then
  the shimmering lines she cannot
name as they dissolve into the sky,
  so lovely that just observing
them is a satisfaction rich
  as the luscious, electric liquid
which is soon to be expressed
  from pomace spread on circular
mats of straw, the pallets stacked
  and squeezed for twenty minutes,
minimum, while unction oozes forth,
  a raw result inducing
tears and green as antifreeze
  at first, but transmuted over
time to achieve its gold-leaf glow,
  composing both the sufficient
means and object of a sort of life—
  of Maria's—the stuff she rations
out upon her daily bread
  (her eyes squinting, her fingers
blistered and aching, after all
  these callused years), the pungent
elegance now on her tongue's tip,
  a nourishment, a custom, an accent,
cultivated residue of time and place,
  this complex and savoring essential.

A NOTE ABOUT THE AUTHOR

George Bradley was born in Roslyn, New York, and was educated at Yale University and the University of Virginia. His first volume of poems, *Terms to Be Met,* was chosen by James Merrill as the winner of the 1985 Yale Younger Poets Prize. Bradley has published two other books of verse, *Of the Knowledge of Good and Evil* and *The Fire Fetched Down,* and he is also the editor of *The Yale Younger Poets Anthology.* Among the awards he has received are the Witter Bynner Prize from the American Academy and Institute of Arts and Letters and the Peter I. B. Lavan Award from the Academy of American Poets. In addition, he has received grants from the National Endowment for the Humanities and the Ingram Merrill Foundation. George Bradley lives near the river of rivers in Chester, Connecticut.

A NOTE ON THE TYPE

The text of this book was set in Scala, a typeface designed by Martin Majoor in 1988 for the Vrendenburg Music Centre in Utrecht for use in their printed matter. Two years later FSI Fontshop International published FF Scala as the first serious text face in the then-new FontFont Library. In 1993 it was augmented with a sans-serif version, also released by FSI.

Composed by NK Graphics,
Keene, New Hampshire
Printed and bound by Edwards Brothers,
Ann Arbor, Michigan
Designed by Virginia Tan